ChordBuddy POP HITS

ISBN 978-1-5400-2579-1

HAL•LEONARD®

Visit Hal Leonard Online at
www.halleonard.com
www.chordbuddy.com

Contact Us:
Hal Leonard
7777 West Bluemound Road
Milwaukee, WI 53213
Email: info@halleonard.com

In Europe contact:
Hal Leonard Europe Limited
Distribution Centre, Newmarket Road
Bury St Edmunds, Suffolk, IP33 3YB
Email: info@halleonardeurope.com

In Australia contact:
Hal Leonard Australia Pty. Ltd.
4 Lentara Court
Cheltenham, Victoria, 3192 Australia
Email: info@halleonard.com.au

Budapest

Words and Music by George Barnett and Joel Pott

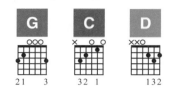

you,   ooh, __   you,   ooh, __ I'd leave it all.
you,   ooh, __   you,   ooh, __ I'd leave it all.
you,   ooh, __   you,   ooh, __ I'd lose it all.

Chorus

Give me one good rea - son why I _____ should nev - er make a change. __

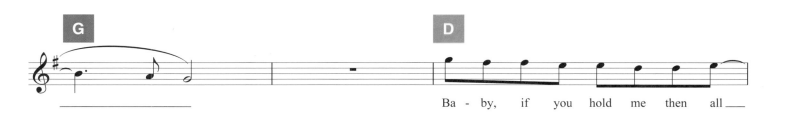

Ba - by, if you hold me then all _____ of this will go _____ a - way. __

Chorus

Give me one good rea - son why I _____ should nev - er make a change. __

_____   Ba - by, if you hold me then all __

__ of this will go _____ a - way. __

Interlude

(Instrumental)

D.S. al Coda
(take 2nd ending)

✪ **Coda**

Outro-Verse

My house in Bu - da - pest; my, ____ my hid - den treas - ure chest; ____

gold - en grand pi - an - o; ____ my beau - ti - ful cas - til - lo: you, ooh, ____

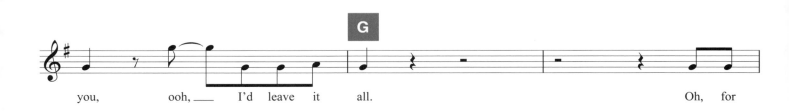

you, ooh, ____ I'd leave it all. Oh, for

you, ooh, ____ you, ooh, ____ I'd leave it all.

Body Like a Back Road

Words and Music by Sam Hunt, Josh Osborne, Shane McAnally and Zach Crowell

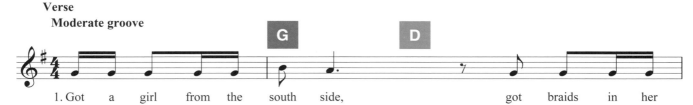

Verse
Moderate groove

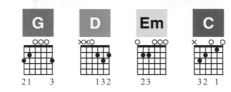

1. Got a girl from the south side, got braids in her hair. First time I seen her walk by, man, I 'bout fell off of my chair. Had to get her number. It took me like six weeks. Now me and her go way back, like Cadillac seats. Bod-y like a

Chorus

back road, drivin' with my eyes closed. I know ev-'ry curve like the back of my hand. ___

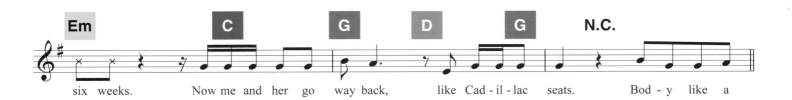

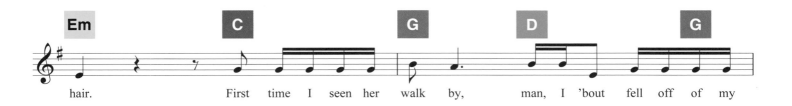

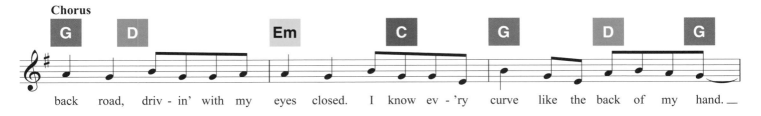

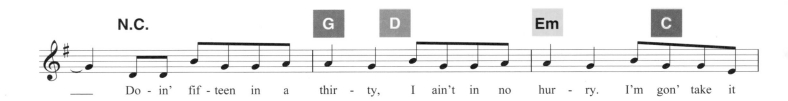

N.C. / G / D / Em / C

Do-in' fif-teen in a thir-ty, I ain't in no hur-ry. I'm gon' take it

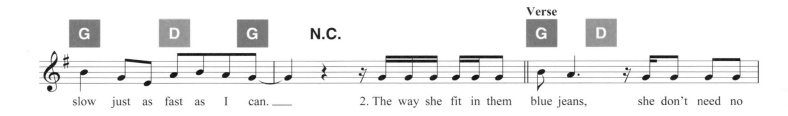

G / D / G / N.C. / **Verse** G / D

slow just as fast as I can. ___ 2. The way she fit in them blue jeans, she don't need no

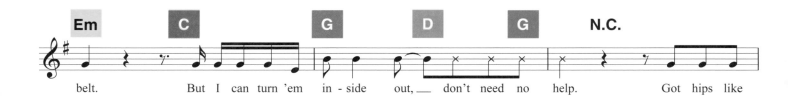

Em / C / G / D / G / N.C.

belt. But I can turn 'em in-side out, ___ don't need no help. Got hips like

G / D / Em / C / G / D / G

hon-ey, so thick and so sweet. There ain't no curves like ___ hers ___ on them down-town

𝄋 Chorus

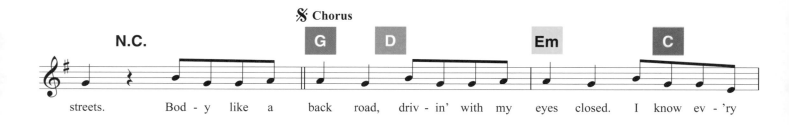

N.C. / G / D / Em / C

streets. Bod-y like a back road, driv-in' with my eyes closed. I know ev-'ry

G / D / G / N.C. / G / D

curve like the back of my hand. ___ Do-in' fif-teen in a thir-ty, I ain't in no

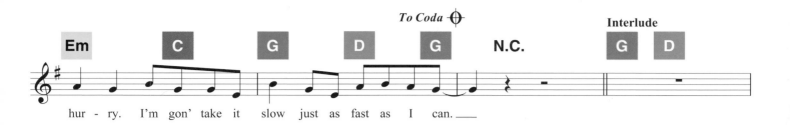

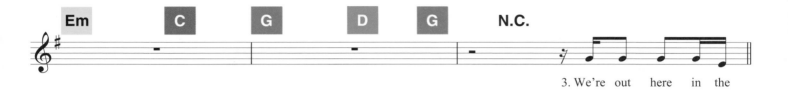

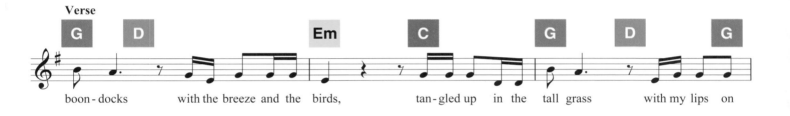

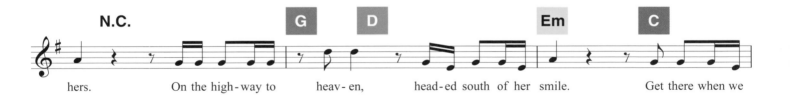

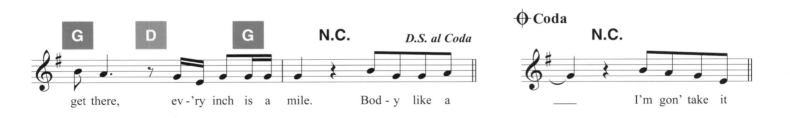

Call Me Maybe

Words and Music by Carly Rae Jepsen, Joshua Ramsay and Tavish Crowe

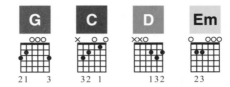

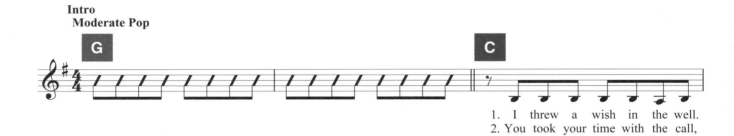

Bridge

Be-fore you came in-to my life, I missed you so bad, I missed you so bad,

I missed you so, so bad. Be-fore you came in-to my life, I missed you so bad.

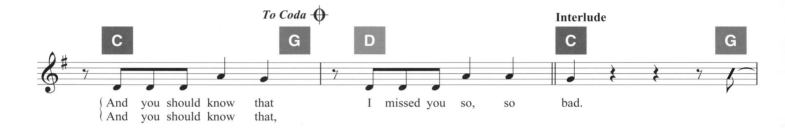

To Coda

Interlude

And you should know that I missed you so, so bad.
And you should know that,

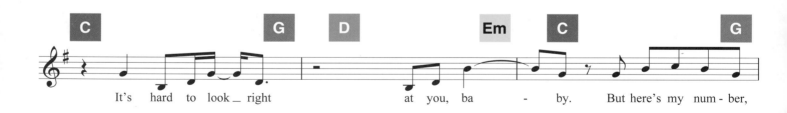

It's hard to look _ right at you, ba - by. But here's my num - ber,

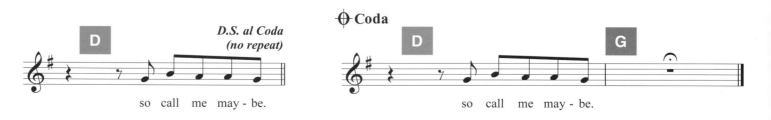

D.S. al Coda
(no repeat)

so call me may - be.

Coda

so call me may - be.

Can't Feel My Face

Words and Music by Abel Tesfaye, Max Martin, Savan Kotecha, Anders Svensson and Ali Payami

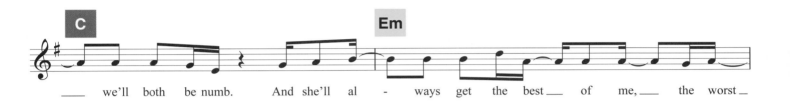

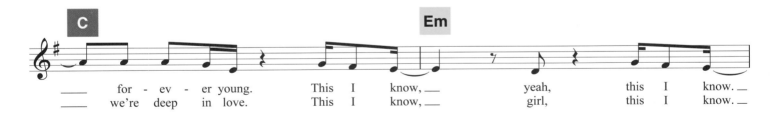

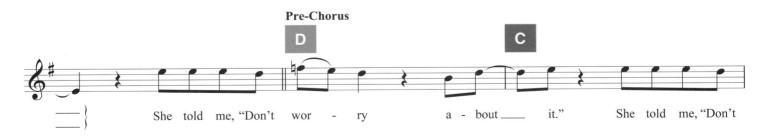

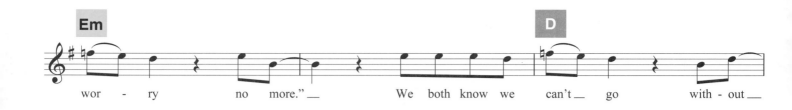

wor - ry no more." ___ We both know we can't ___ go with - out ___

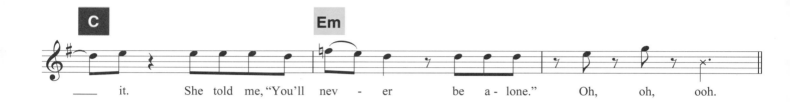

___ it. She told me, "You'll nev - er be a - lone." Oh, oh, ooh.

Chorus

I can't feel my face when I'm with you, but I love ___ it, but I love ___

___ it. Oh. ___ I can't feel my face when I'm with you, but I love ___

1.

2., 3.

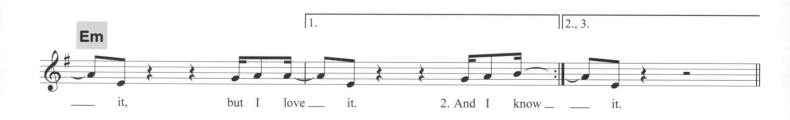

___ it, but I love ___ it. 2. And I know ___ ___ it.

Chorus

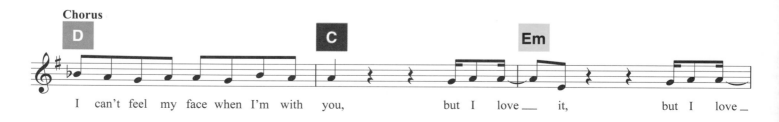

I can't feel my face when I'm with you, but I love ___ it, but I love ___

it. Oh. __ I can't feel my face when I'm with you, but I love __

__ it, but I love __ it. Oh. __

Pre-Chorus

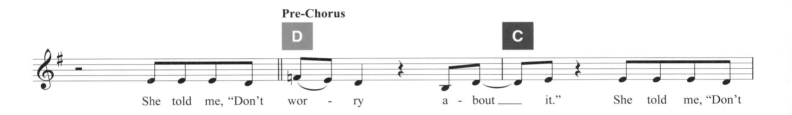

She told me, "Don't wor - ry a - bout __ it." She told me, "Don't

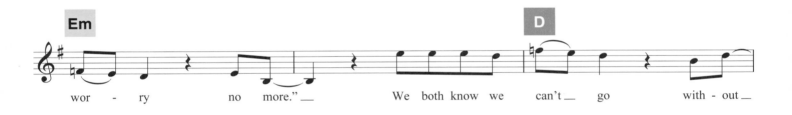

wor - ry no more." __ We both know we can't __ go with - out __

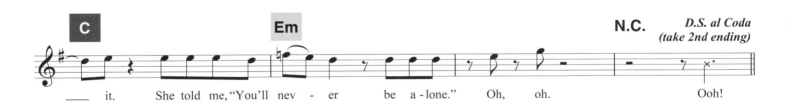

N.C. *D.S. al Coda (take 2nd ending)*

__ it. She told me, "You'll nev - er be a - lone." Oh, oh. Ooh!

⊕ Coda **Outro**

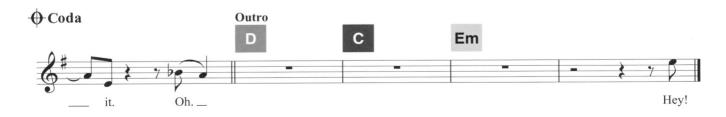

__ it. Oh. __ Hey!

Chasing Cars

Words and Music by Gary Lightbody, Tom Simpson, Paul Wilson, Jonathan Quinn and Nathan Connolly

Closer

Words and Music by Andrew Taggart, Isaac Slade, Joseph King,
Ashley Frangipane, Shaun Frank and Frederic Kennett

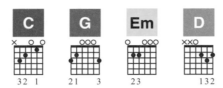

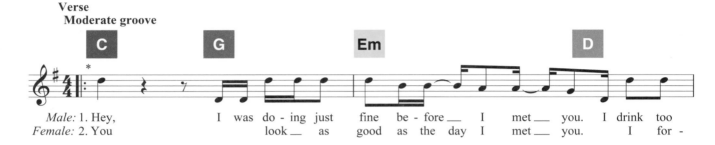

Male: 1. Hey, I was do-ing just fine be-fore ___ I met ___ you. I drink too
Female: 2. You look ___ as good as the day I met ___ you. I for-

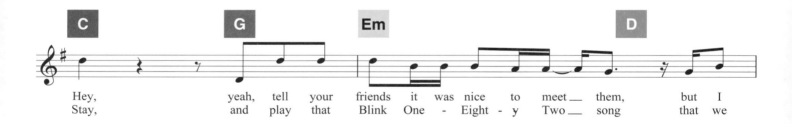

much, and that's ___ an is-sue, but I'm o-kay.
get just why ___ I left you; I was in-sane.

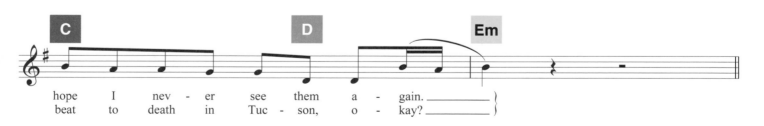

Hey, yeah, tell your friends it was nice to meet ___ them, but I
Stay, and play that Blink One - Eight-y Two ___ song that we

hope I nev-er see them a - gain. _____
beat to death in Tuc-son, o - kay? _____

* Vocal written an octave higher than sung.

Pre-Chorus

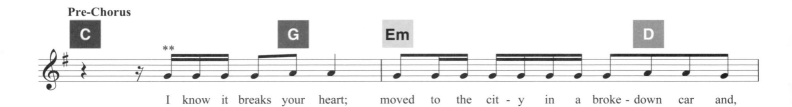

I know it breaks your heart; moved to the cit-y in a broke-down car and,

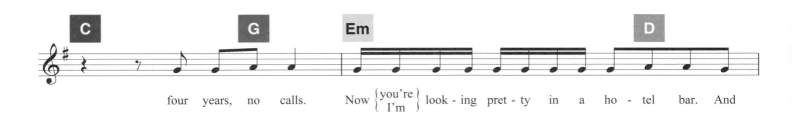

four years, no calls. Now {you're / I'm} look-ing pret-ty in a ho-tel bar. And

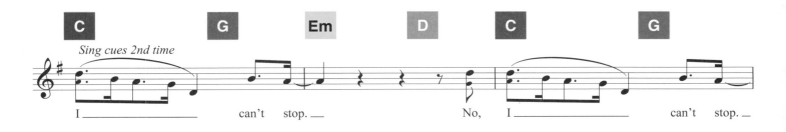

Sing cues 2nd time

I _____ can't stop. __ No, I _____ can't stop. __

Chorus

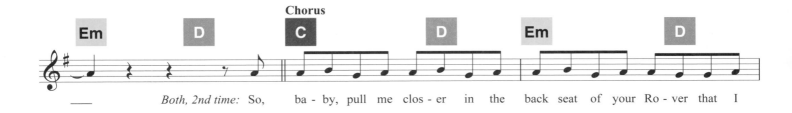

_____ *Both, 2nd time:* So, ba-by, pull me clos-er in the back seat of your Ro-ver that I

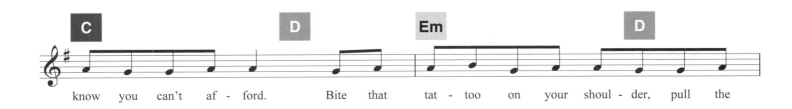

know you can't af-ford. Bite that tat-too on your shoul-der, pull the

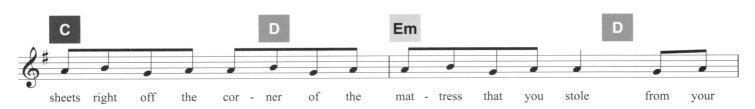

sheets right off the cor-ner of the mat-tress that you stole from your

** *Vocal written at sung pitch.*

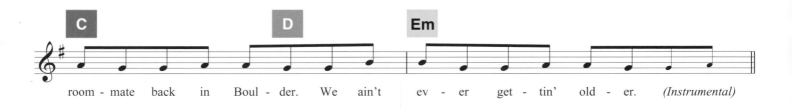
room - mate back in Boul - der. We ain't ev - er get - tin' old - er. *(Instrumental)*

Interlude

We ain't

ev - er get - tin' old - er. *(Instrumental)*

We ain't ev - er get - tin' old - er.   ev - er get - tin' old - er. *Male:* So,

Chorus

ba - by, pull me clos - er in the back seat of your Ro - ver that I know you can't af - ford. Bite that

tat - too on your shoul - der, pull the sheets right off the cor - ner of the mat - tress that you stole from your

20

room - mate back in Boul - der. We ain't ev - er get - tin' old - er. We ain't ev - er get - tin' old - er. We ain't
Female: We ain't

ev - er get - tin' old - er. We ain't ev - er get - tin' old - er. We ain't ev - er get - tin' old - er. We ain't
ev - er get - tin' old - er.   *Female:* No, we ain't ev - er get - tin' old - er.

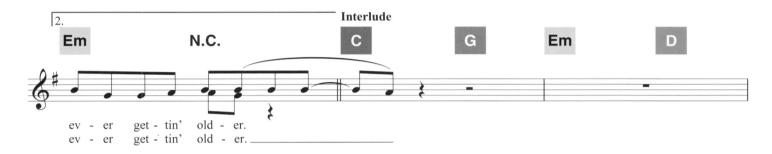

ev - er get - tin' old - er.
ev - er get - tin' old - er. _____

Both: We ain't ev - er get - tin' old - er.

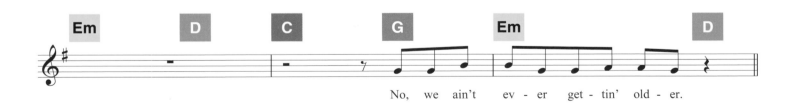

No, we ain't ev - er get - tin' old - er.

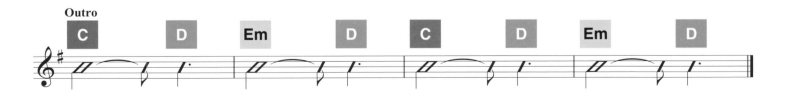

Cruise

Words and Music by Chase Rice, Tyler Hubbard, Brian Kelley, Joey Moi and Jesse Rice

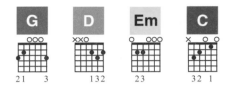

Intro
Moderately, in 2

Ba - by, you a song. You make me wan - na roll ___ my win - dows down and

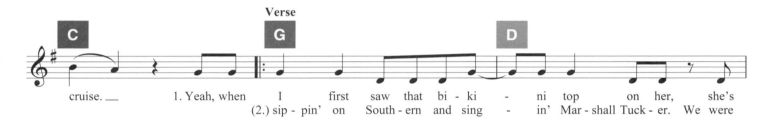

cruise. ___ 1. Yeah, when I first saw that bi - ki - ni top on her, she's
(2.) sip - pin' on South - ern and sing - in' Mar - shall Tuck - er. We were

pop - pin' right out - ta the South ___ Geor - gia wa - ter. Thought, "Oh, ___ good Lord!" ___ She had them
fall - in' in love in the sweet ___ heart of sum - mer. She hopped right up ___ in - to the

long, tanned legs. Could - n't help my - self, so I walked up and said:
cab of my truck and said, "Fire it up, let's go get this thing stuck." Well,

Chorus

ba - by, you a song. You make me wan - na roll my win - dows down and cruise ___ down a

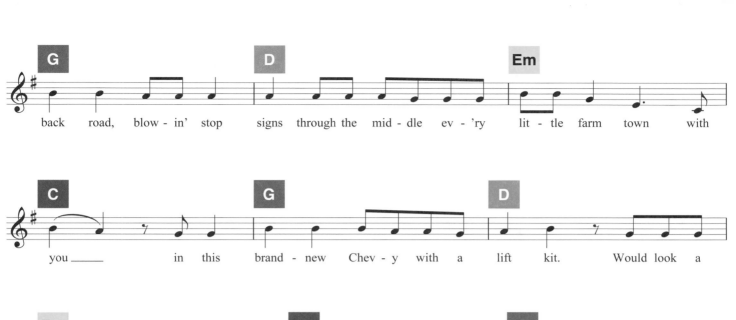

back road, blow-in' stop signs through the mid-dle ev-'ry lit-tle farm town with

you _____ in this brand-new Chev-y with a lift kit. Would look a

hell of a lot bet-ter with you up in it. So, ba-by, you a song. You

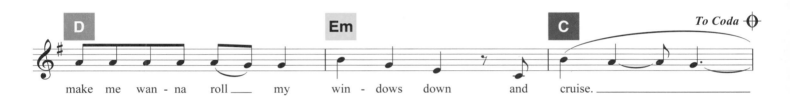

make me wan-na roll _____ my win-dows down and cruise. _____

To Coda ⊕

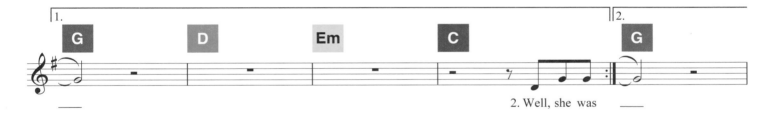

1.

2.
2. Well, she was _____

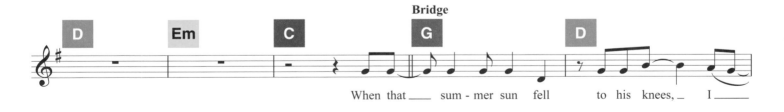

Bridge

When that _____ sum-mer sun fell to his knees, _ I _____

_____ looked at her and she _____ looked at me and I turned on those

Hey, Soul Sister

Words and Music by Pat Monahan, Espen Lind and Amund Bjorklund

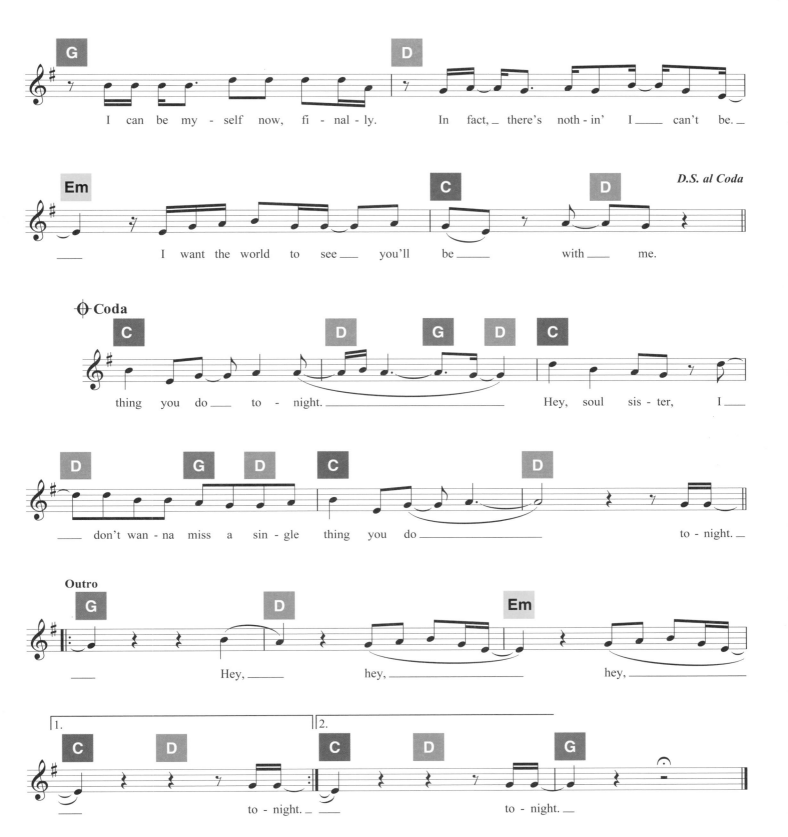

Additional Lyrics

2. Just in time, I'm so glad you have a one-track mind like me.
   You gave my life direction,
   A game-show love connection we can't deny.
   I'm so obsessed, my heart is bound to beat right out my un-trimmed chest.
   I believe in you. Like a virgin, you're Madonna
   And I'm always gonna wanna blow your mind.

Despacito

Words and Music by Luis Fonsi, Erika Ender, Justin Bieber,
Jason Boyd, Marty James Garton and Ramón Ayala

Verse
Moderate Latin beat, in 2

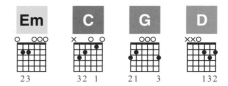

I Gotta Feeling

Words and Music by Will Adams, Allan Pineda, Jaime Gomez, Stacy Ferguson, David Guetta and Frederic Riesterer

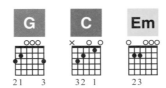

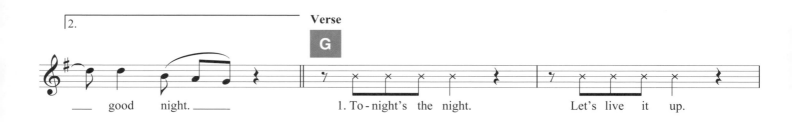

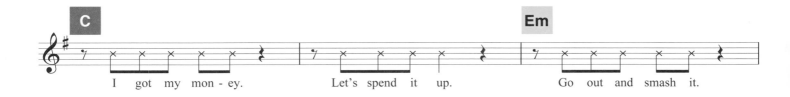

I got my mon - ey. Let's spend it up. Go out and smash it.

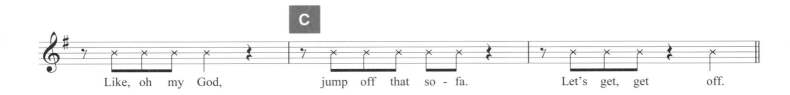

Like, oh my God, jump off that so - fa. Let's get, get off.

Bridge

I _____ know that we'll _____ have a ball _____ if we get _____

_____ down and go _____ out and just _____ lose it all. _____ I feel

stressed _____ out. I wan - na let go. Let's go way _____ out, spaced _____ out and los -

Verse

ing all con - trol. (Ch - ch - ch - ch.) 2. Fill up my cup. Ma - zel tov!

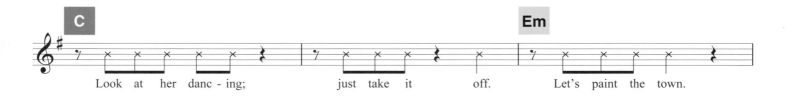

Look at her danc-ing; just take it off. Let's paint the town.

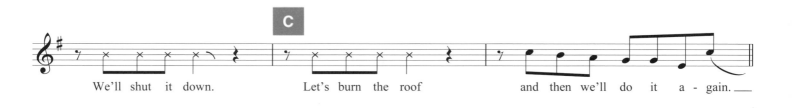

We'll shut it down. Let's burn the roof and then we'll do it a-gain. ___

Pre-Chorus

___ Let's do it, let's do it, let's do it, let's do

it, ___ and do it, and do it. Let's live it up, and do it, and do it, and

D.S. al Coda
(with repeat)

do it, do it, do it. Let's do it. Let's do it. Let's do it, 'cause I got-ta feel-

⊕ Coda

___ good night. _____ (Woo hoo.)

Ho Hey

Words and Music by Jeremy Fraites and Wesley Schultz

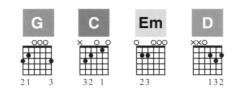

Verse
Moderately slow, in 2

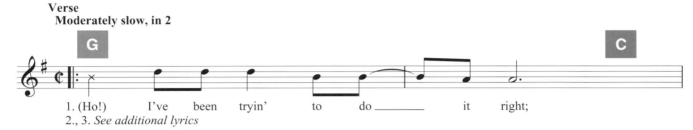

1. (Ho!) I've been tryin' to do _____ it right;
2., 3. *See additional lyrics*

(Hey!) I've been liv-in' a lone - ly life. _____ (Ho!) I've been sleep - in' here _____

_____ in - stead; (Hey!) I've been sleep - in' in _____ my bed, _____

To Coda 1 ⊕ | 1.

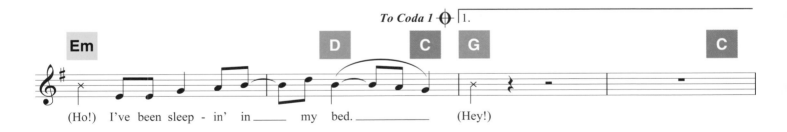

(Ho!) I've been sleep - in' in _____ my bed. _____ (Hey!)

| 2.

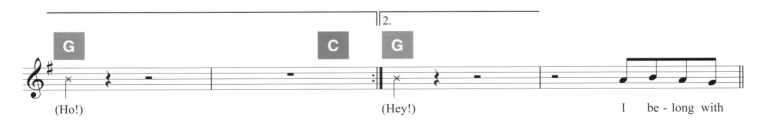

(Ho!) (Hey!) I be - long with

% Chorus

Em ... **D** ... **G**

you, you be-long with me; you're my ___ sweet - heart. ___

Em ... **D** ... **C**

I be - long with you, you be - long with me; you're my ___ sweet -

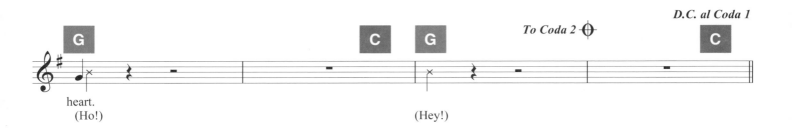

G ... **C G** ... *To Coda 2* ... *D.C. al Coda 1* ... **C**

heart. (Hey!)
(Ho!)

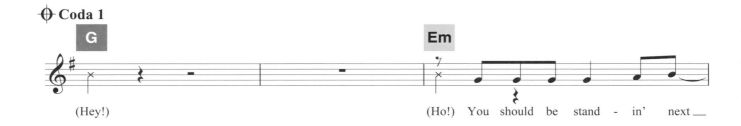

⊕ **Coda 1**

G ... **Em**

(Hey!) (Ho!) You should be stand - in' next ___

D ... **C G**

___ to me. ___ (Hey!) I be - long with

Chorus

Em ... **D** ... **G**

you, you be - long with me; you're my ___ sweet - heart. ___

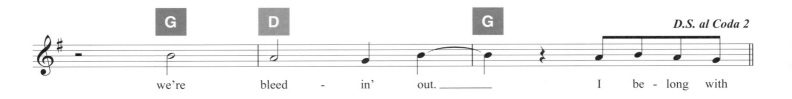

Additional Lyrics

2. (Ho!) So show me, family,
   (Hey!) All the blood that I will bleed.
   (Ho!) I don't know where I belong,
   (Hey!) I don't know where I went wrong,
   (Ho!) But I can write a song.
   (Hey!)

3. (Ho!) I don't think you're right for him.
   (Hey!) Look at what it might have been if you
   (Ho!) Took a bus to Chinatown.
   (Hey!) I'd be standing on Canal
   (Ho!) And Bowery. *(To Coda 1)*

Issues

Words and Music by Benjamin Levin, Mikkel Eriksen, Tor Hermansen, Julia Michaels and Justin Tranter

I Knew You Were Trouble

Words and Music by Taylor Swift, Shellback and Max Martin

gone   when he's next _____ to _____
gone   when he met _____

me,   and I re   -   a - lize _____ the blame is on _____
me,   and I re   -   a - lize _____ the joke is on _____

𝄋 **Chorus**

me. _____   'Cause I knew you were trou-ble when you walked in, _____ so
me. _____

shame on me now. _____ Flew me to plac - es I'd nev - er been _____

till you put me down. Oh, I knew you were

trou - ble when you walked in, _____ so shame on me now. _____

_____ Flew me to plac - es I'd nev - er been. _____ Now I'm

Just the Way You Are

Words and Music by Bruno Mars, Ari Levine, Philip Lawrence, Khari Cain and Khalil Walton

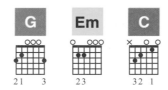

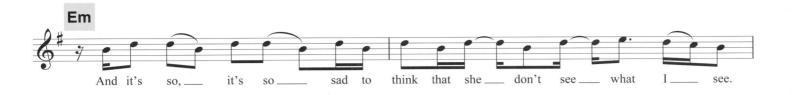

And it's so,___ it's so___ sad to think that she___ don't see___ what I___ see.

But ev-'ry time___ she asks___ me, "Do___ I look___ o - kay?"___ I___ say:___

𝄋 Chorus

When I see your face,___ there's not a thing___

___ that I___ would change, ___ 'cause you're a - maz - ing ___ just ___ the way___ you are.___

And when you smile, ___ the whole world stops ___

___ and stares ___ for a while, ___ 'cause, girl, you're a - maz - ing _____ just___

To Coda ✛

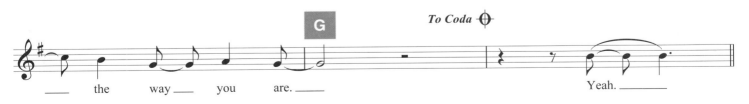

___ the way ___ you are. ___ Yeah.___

Verse

2. Her lips, ___ her lips, ___ I could kiss them all ___ day if ___ she'd let me.

Her laugh, ___ her laugh, ___ she hates but I ___ think it's ___ so sex - y.

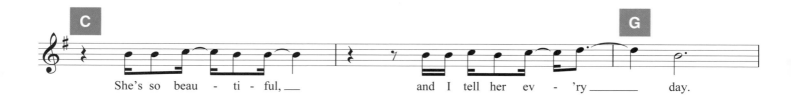

She's so beau - ti - ful, ___ and I tell her ev - 'ry ___ day.

Oh, you know, you know, you know I'd nev - er ask you to change. ___ If

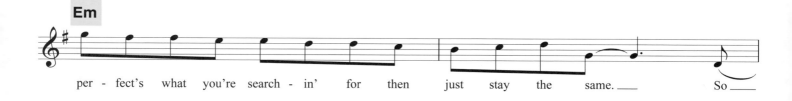

per - fect's what you're search - in' for then just stay the same. ___ So ___

___ don't e - ven both - er ask - in' if ___ you look ___ o - kay. ___ You know I'll

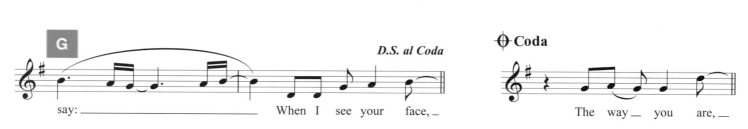

D.S. al Coda

say: _____ When I see your face, ___

⊕ **Coda**

The way ___ you are, ___

Love on the Weekend

Words and Music by John Mayer

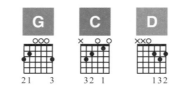

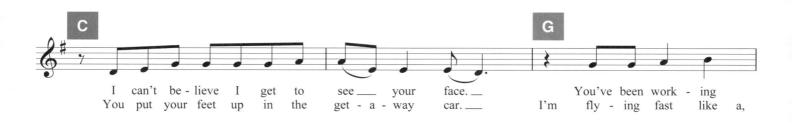

1. It's a Fri - day; we fi - n'lly made it.
2. You be the D. J., I'll be the driv - er.

I can't be - lieve I get to see ___ your face. ___ You've been work - ing
You put your feet up in the get - a - way car. ___ I'm fly - ing fast like a,

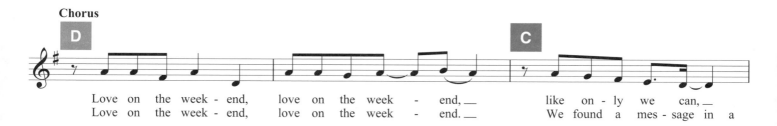

and I've been wait - ing to pick you up and take you from this place. ___
a want - ed man. I want you, ba - by, like you can't ___ un - der - stand. ___

Chorus

Love on the week - end, love on the week - end, ___ like on - ly we can, ___
Love on the week - end, love on the week - end. ___ We found a mes - sage in a

like on - ly we can. ___ Love on the week - end, love on the week - end. ___
bot - tle we were drink - ing. Love on the week - end, love on the week - end. ___

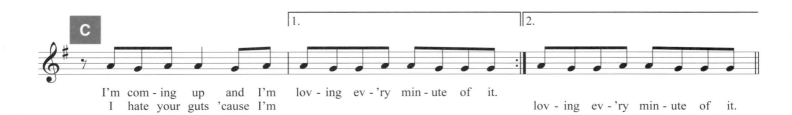

I'm com - ing up and I'm lov - ing ev - 'ry min - ute of it.
I hate your guts 'cause I'm lov - ing ev - 'ry min - ute of it.

Interlude

Oh, _____ oh, _____

oh, _____ oh. _____

Verse

3. I got - ta leave ya; it's gon - na hurt me.

My clothes are dirt - y and my friends are get - ting wor - ried. Down there be - low us,

un - der the clouds, ba - by, take my hand and pull me down, down, down, down.

Chorus 2

And I'll be dream-ing of the next time we can go ___ in - to an - oth - er ser - o -

to - nin o - ver-flow. Love on the week - end, love on the week - end. ___

Outro

I'm bust-ed up, but I'm lov-ing ev - 'ry min - ute of it. *(Instrumental)*

Love on ___ the week - end. ___

Love on ___ the week - end. ___

Million Reasons

Words and Music by Stefani Germanotta, Mark Ronson and Hillary Lindsey

Verse
Moderately slow, in 2

1. You're giv - in' me a mil - lion rea - sons to let you go. _____ You're
2. Head stuck in a cy - cle, I look off and I stare. _____ It's

giv - in' me a mil - lion rea - sons to quit the show. _____ You're
like that I've stopped breath - in' but com - plete - ly a - ware. _____ 'Cause you're

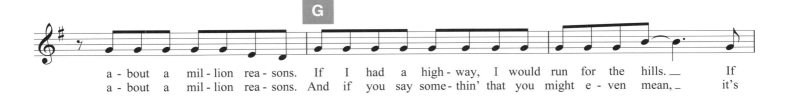

giv - in' me a mil - lion rea - sons, give me a mil - lion rea - sons. Giv - in' me a mil - lion rea - sons,
giv - in' me a mil - lion rea - sons, give me a mil - lion rea - sons. Giv - in' me a mil - lion rea - sons,

a - bout a mil - lion rea - sons. If I had a high - way, I would run for the hills. _____ If
a - bout a mil - lion rea - sons. And if you say some - thin' that you might e - ven mean, _ it's

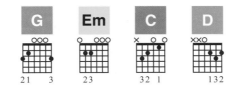

you could find a dry way, I'd for - ev - er be still. _____ But you're)
hard to e - ven fath - om which parts I should be - lieve. _____ 'Cause you're)

giv - in' me a mil - lion rea - sons, give me a mil - lion rea - sons. Giv - in' me a mil - lion rea - sons,

%. Chorus

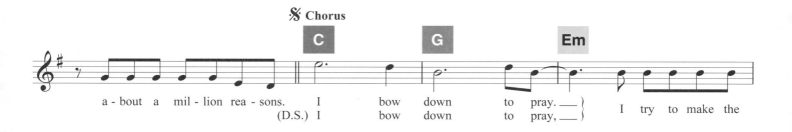

a - bout a mil - lion rea - sons. I bow down to pray. —
(D.S.) I bow down to pray, — I try to make the

worst seem bet - ter. — Lord, show me the way — to cut through all this

worn - out leath - er. I've got a hun - dred mil - lion rea - sons to walk a - way, —

1.

To Coda ⊕

but, ba - by, I just need one good one — to stay. —

2.   **Bridge**

good one — to stay. —

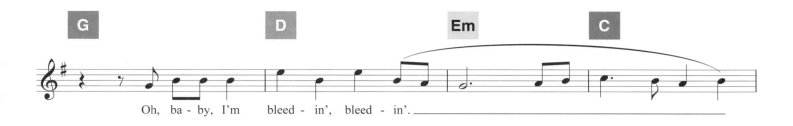
Oh, ba-by, I'm bleed-in', bleed-in'. ___

Can't you give me what I'm need-in', need-in'? Ev - 'ry heart-break makes it

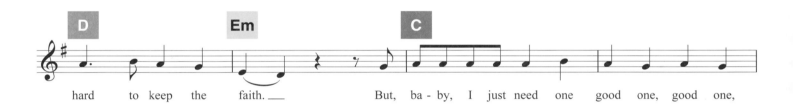
hard to keep the faith. ___ But, ba-by, I just need one good one, good one,

D.S. al Coda   **Coda**

good one, good one, good one, good one. When   good one, good one.

Outro

Tell me that you'll be the good one, good one. Ba - by, I just need one

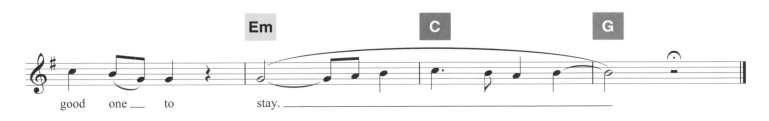
good one ___ to stay. ___

Perfect

Words and Music by Ed Sheeran

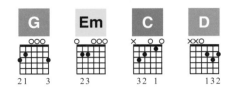

Verse
Classic Ballad

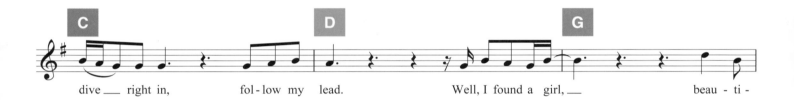

1. I found a love ___ for ___ me. ___ Dar-ling, just

dive ___ right in, fol-low my lead. Well, I found a girl, ___ beau-ti-

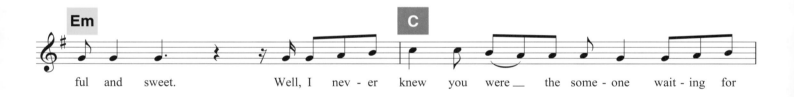

ful and sweet. Well, I nev-er knew you were ___ the some-one wait-ing for

me. ___ 'Cause we were just kids when we | fell ___ in ___ love, not know-ing
so ___ in ___ love, fight-ing a-

what ___ it was. I will not give you ___ up this
gainst ___ all odds. I know we'll be all ___ right this

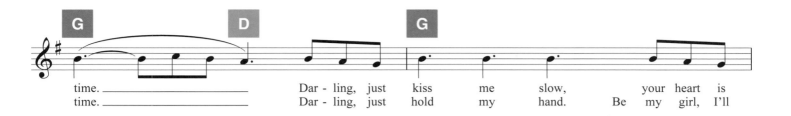

time. _____ Dar - ling, just kiss me slow, your heart is
time. _____ Dar - ling, just hold my hand. Be my girl, I'll

all _____ I _____ own. And in your eyes, you're _____ hold - ing mine. _____
be _____ your _____ man. I've seen the fu - ture _____ in your eyes. _____

Chorus

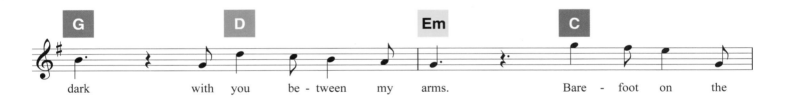

_____ } Ba - by, _____ I'm danc - ing in the

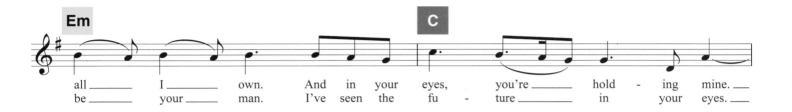

dark with you be - tween my arms. Bare - foot on the

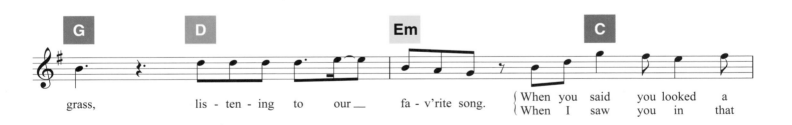

grass, lis - ten - ing to our _____ fa - v'rite song. { When you said you looked a
{ When I saw you in that

To Coda ⊕

mess, I whis - pered un - der - neath my breath. But you heard it, "Dar - ling,
dress, look - ing so beau - ti - ful, I don't _____ de - serve this. "Dar - ling,

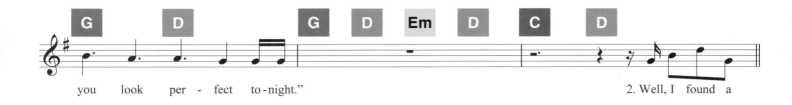

you look per - fect to-night."   2. Well, I found a

Verse

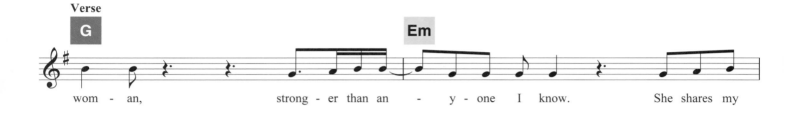

wom - an,   strong - er than an - y - one I know.   She shares my

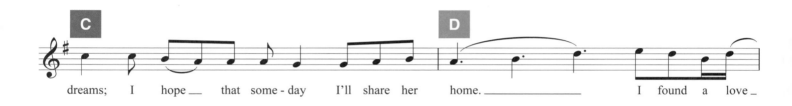

dreams; I hope ___ that some - day I'll share her home._____   I found a love ___

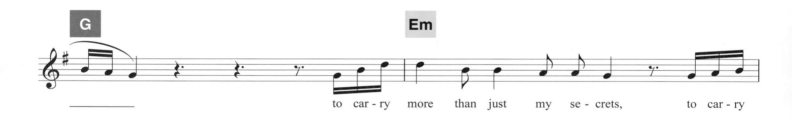

___   to car - ry more than just my se - crets,   to car - ry

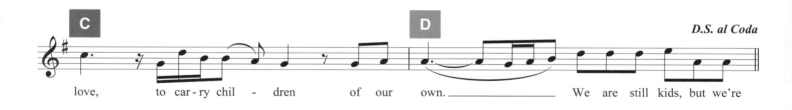

D.S. al Coda

love, to car - ry chil - dren of our own._____   We are still kids, but we're

Coda

Interlude

you look per - fect to - night."

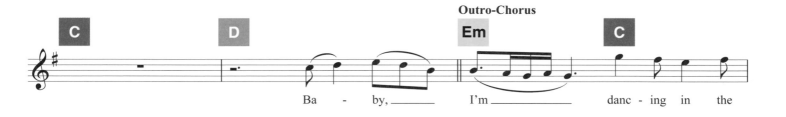

Outro-Chorus

Ba - by, _____ I'm _____ danc - ing in the

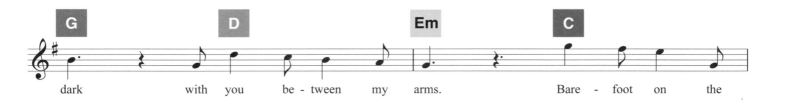

dark with you be - tween my arms. Bare - foot on the

grass, lis - ten - ing to our ___ fa - v'rite song. I have faith in what ___ I

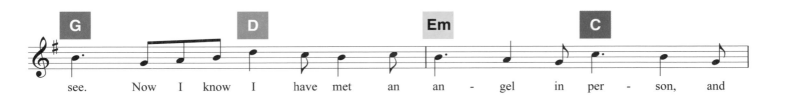

see. Now I know I have met an an - gel in per - son, and

she looks per - fect. I don't de - serve this, you look per - fect to - night.

Riptide

Words and Music by Vance Joy

rip - tide, tak-en a-way ___ to the dark side, I wan-na be ___ your

left-hand ___ man. ___ I love you when you're sing - ing that

song, ___ and I got a lump ___ in my throat 'cause you're gon-na sing ___ the words ___

1. ___ wrong.   2. ___ wrong.   (Instrumental)

Bridge

I just wan - na, I just wan - na know ___ if you're gon - na, if you're gon - na stay. ___

I just got - ta, I just got - ta know; ___

I can't have ___ it, I can't have ___ it an - y oth - er way. I swear she's des - tined for the

screen; clos - est thing to Mi - chelle Pfeif - fer that you've ev - er seen. Oh, __

Chorus

la - dy, __ run - ning down __ to the rip - tide, tak - en a - way __ to the

dark side, I wan - na be __ your left - hand __ man. __ I

love you when you're sing - ing that song, __ and I got a lump __ in my

1., 2.

throat 'cause you're gon - na sing __ the words __ wrong. Oh,

3.

throat 'cause you're gon - na sing __ the words wrong, and __ I got a lump __ in my

throat 'cause you're gon - na sing __ the words __ wrong.

Praying

Words and Music by Kesha Sebert, Ben Abraham, Ryan Lewis and Andrew Joslyn

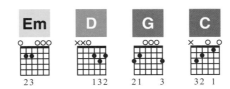

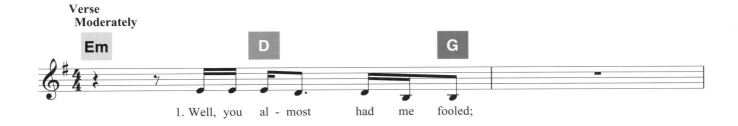

Verse
Moderately

1. Well, you al - most had me fooled;

told me that I was ___ noth - ing with - out you. ___ Oh, ___

___ but af - ter ev - 'ry - thing ___ you've done,

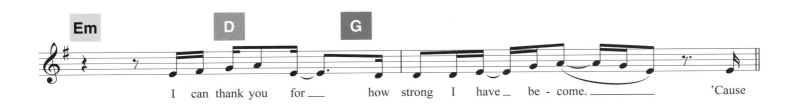

I can thank you for ___ how strong I have ___ be - come. _____ 'Cause

Pre-Chorus

you brought the flames and you put me through hell. I had to learn how to fight for my-self.

And we both know all the truth I could tell. I'll just say this is "I wish you fare-well."___

Chorus

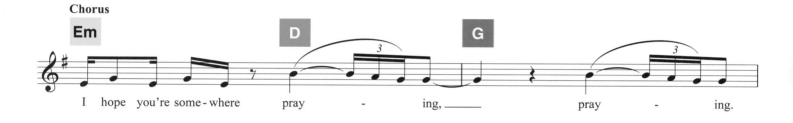

I hope you're some-where pray - ing,___ pray - ing.

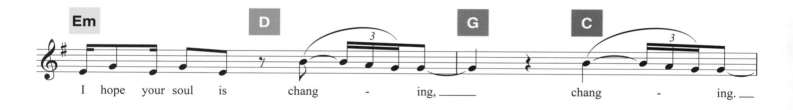

I hope your soul is chang - ing,___ chang - ing. __

___ I hope you find your peace __ fall - ing on __ your knees, __

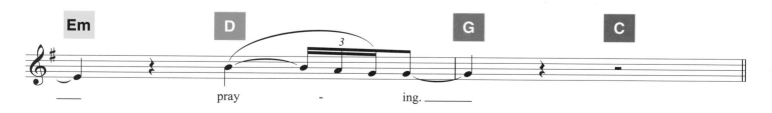

___ pray - ing. ___

Verse

2. I'm proud of who I am.

No more mon - sters; I can breathe a - gain. _____

And you said that I was done. _____

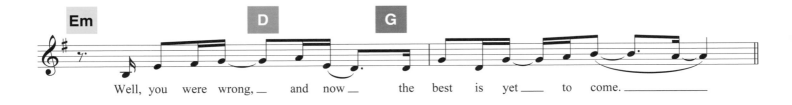

Well, you were wrong, __ and now __ the best is yet __ to come. _____

Bridge

'Cause I can make it on __ my own, _____ oh.

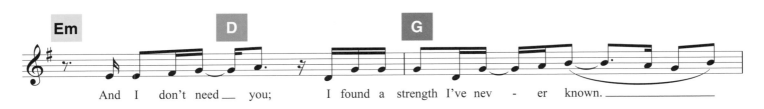

And I don't need __ you; I found a strength I've nev - er known. _____

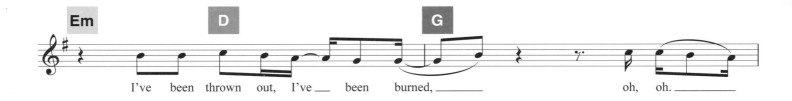

I've been thrown out, I've __ been burned, _____ oh, oh. _____

When I'm fin-ished, they won't e-ven know __ your name. _____

Pre-Chorus

You brought the flames and you put me through hell. I had to learn how to fight for my-self.

And we both know all the truth I could tell. __ I'll just say this is "I wish you fare-well." __

𝄋 Chorus

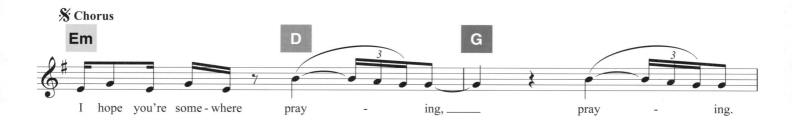

I hope you're some-where pray - ing, _____ pray - ing.

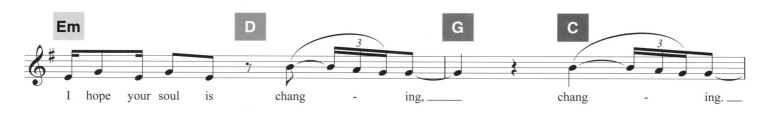

I hope your soul is chang - ing, _____ chang - ing. __

66

I hope you find your peace ____ fall - ing on ____ your knees, ____

To Coda ⊕

Bridge

____ pray - ing. ____ Oh, some - times I pray for you at night, ____

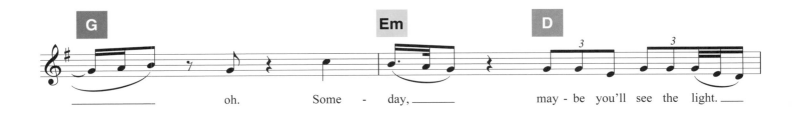

____ oh. Some - day, ____ may - be you'll see the light. ____

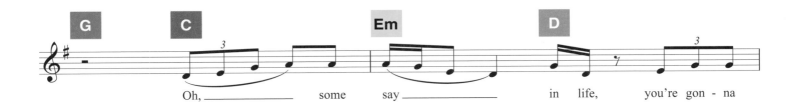

Oh, ____ some say ____ in life, you're gon - na

D.S. al Coda

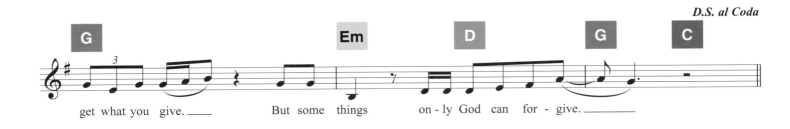

get what you give. ____ But some things on - ly God can for - give. ____

⊕ **Coda**

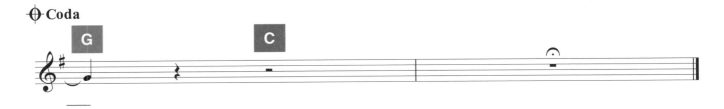

Rude

Words and Music by Nasri Atweh, Mark Pellizzer, Alex Tanas, Ben Spivak and Adam Messinger

Royals

Words and Music by Ella Yelich-O'Connor and Joel Little

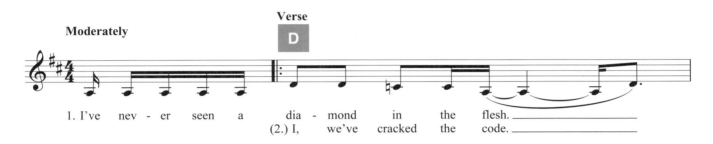

Moderately

Verse
D

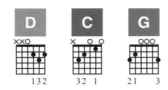

1. I've nev-er seen a dia-mond in the flesh. _____
(2.) I, we've cracked the code. _____

I cut my teeth on wed-ding rings _____ in the
We count our dol-lars on the train _____ to the

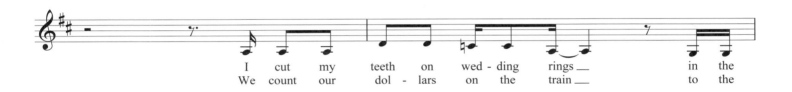

mov-ies. _____ And I'm not proud of my ad-dress. _____
par-ty. _____ And ev-'ry-one who knows us knows _____

In the torn-up town, no post-code
that we're fine with this. We did-n't come from

Pre-Chorus
D

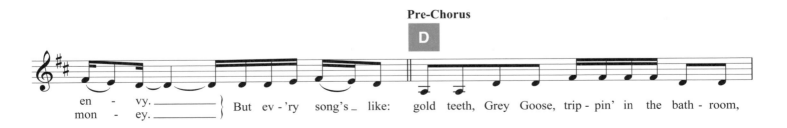

en-vy. _____
mon-ey. _____ } But ev-'ry song's _ like: gold teeth, Grey Goose, trip-pin' in the bath-room,

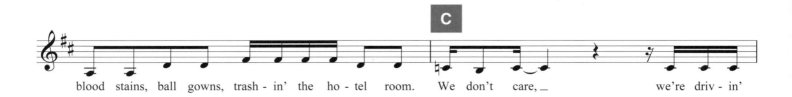

blood stains, ball gowns, trash-in' the ho-tel room. We don't care, __ we're driv-in'

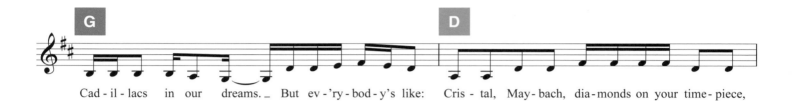

Cad-il-lacs in our dreams. __ But ev-'ry-bod-y's like: Cris-tal, May-bach, dia-monds on your time-piece,

jet planes, is-lands, ti-gers on a gold leash. We don't care, __ we aren't

caught up in your love af-fair. __ And we'll nev-er be roy-als, (roy-als.)

It don't run in our __ blood. __ That kind of luxe just ain't __ for us. __ We crave a

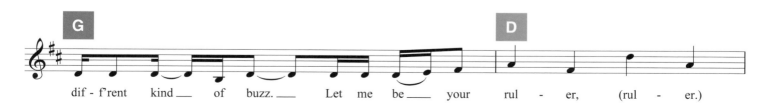

dif-f'rent kind __ of buzz. __ Let me be __ your rul-er, (rul-er.)

72

You can call me queen bee and, ba - by, I'll rule, I'll rule, I'll rule, I'll rule.

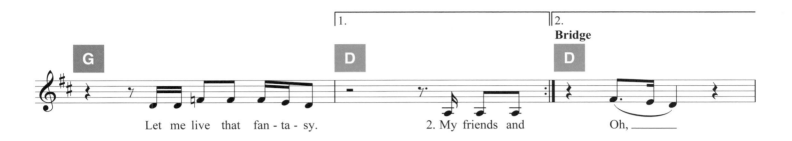

Let me live that fan - ta - sy.   2. My friends and   Oh, _____

oh, _____   oh, _____   we're big - ger than we ev - er dreamed. _____

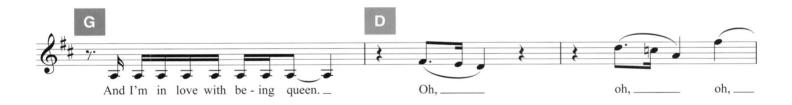

And I'm in love with be - ing queen. _____   Oh, _____   oh, _____   oh, _____

_____ life is game with - out a care. _____ We aren't caught up in your love af - fair. _____ And we'll nev - er be

$\oplus$ **Coda**

Let me live that fan - ta - sy.

Send My Love
(To Your New Lover)

Words and Music by Adele Adkins, Max Martin and Shellback

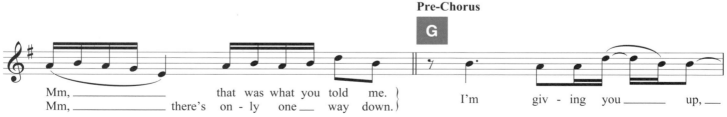

Shattered
(Turn the Car Around)

Words and Music by Gregg Wattenberg and Marc Roberge

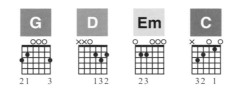

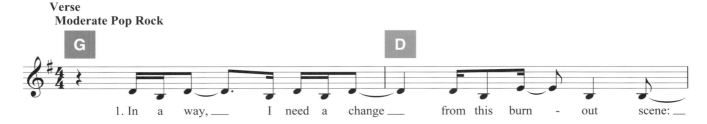

Verse
Moderate Pop Rock

1. In a way, ___ I need a change ___ from this burn - out scene: ___

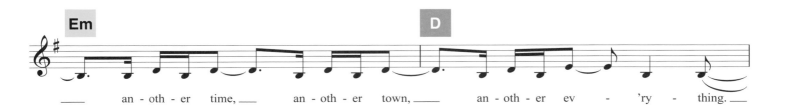

___ an - oth - er time, ___ an - oth - er town, ___ an - oth - er ev - 'ry - thing. ___

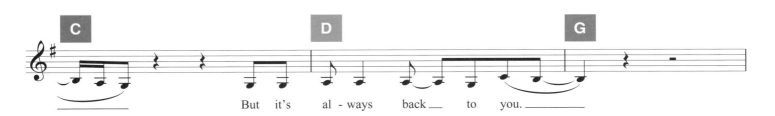

But it's al - ways back ___ to you. ___

Verse

2. Stum - ble out ___ in the night ___
3. I had no i - dea ___ that the night ___

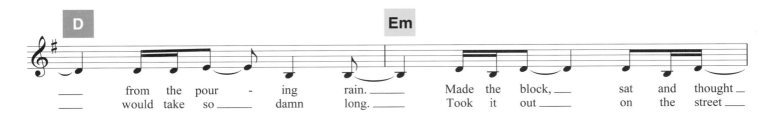

from the pour - ing rain. ___ Made the block, ___ sat and thought
would take so ___ damn long. ___ Took it out ___ on the street

Sign of the Times

Words and Music by Harry Styles, Jeffrey Bhasker, Alex Salibian, Tyler Johnson, Mitch Rowland and Ryan Nasci

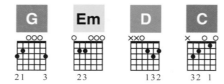

Verse
Moderately slow, in 2

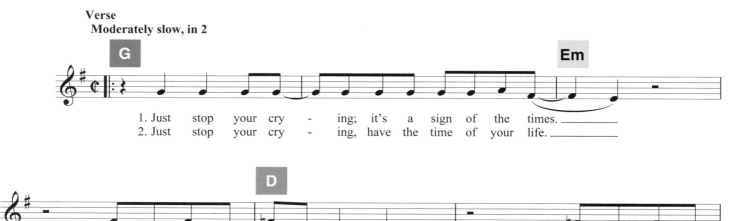

1. Just stop your cry - ing; it's a sign of the times. _____
2. Just stop your cry - ing, have the time of your life. _____

Wel - come to the fi - nal show. Hope you're wear - ing
Break - ing through the at - mos - phere, and things are pret - ty

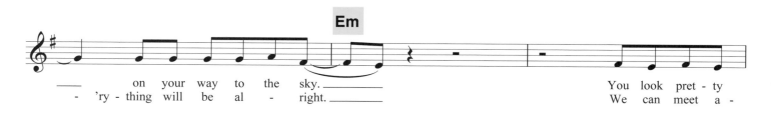

your ___ best clothes. You can't bribe the door ___
good ___ from here. Re - mem - ber, ev -

on your way to the sky. _____ You look pret - ty
- 'ry - thing will be al - right. _____ We can meet a -

good ___ down here, but you ain't real - ly good. ___
gain ___ some - where, some - where far a - way ___ from here.

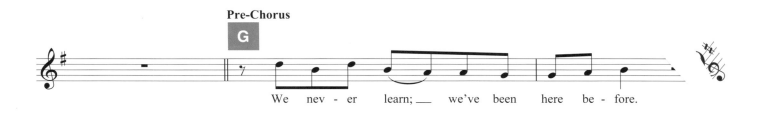

Pre-Chorus
We nev-er learn; we've been here be-fore.

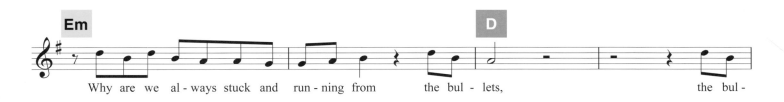

Why are we al-ways stuck and run-ning from the bul-lets, the bul-

lets? We nev-er learn; we been here be-fore.

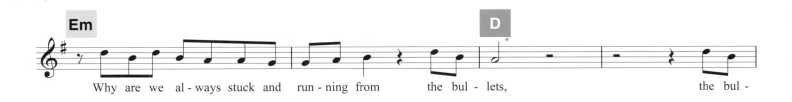

Why are we al-ways stuck and run-ning from the bul-lets, the bul-

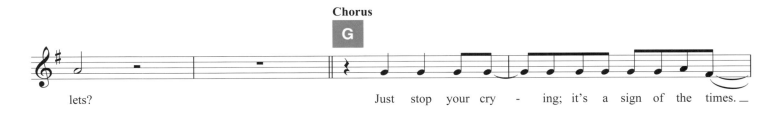

Chorus
lets? Just stop your cry - ing; it's a sign of the times.

We got-ta get a - way from here.

We got-ta get a - way from here. Just stop your cry - / Stop your cry-ing, ba-

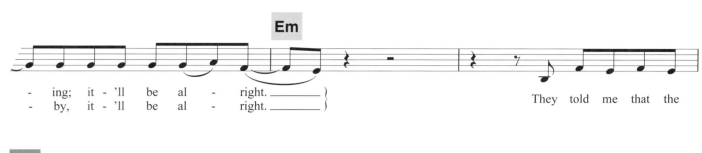

Stay with Me

Words and Music by Sam Smith, James Napier, William Edward Phillips, Tom Petty and Jeff Lynne

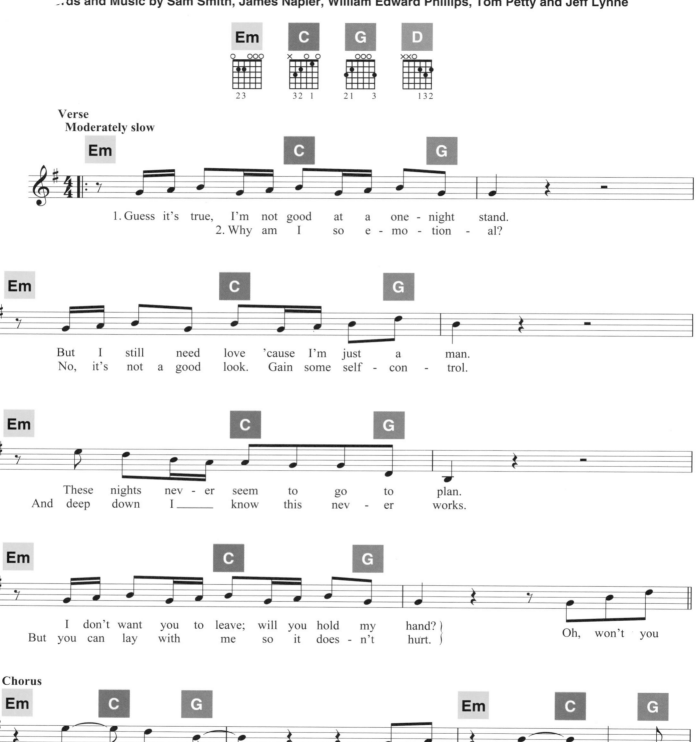

Use Somebody

Words and Music by Caleb Followill, Nathan Followill, Jared Followill and Matthew Followill

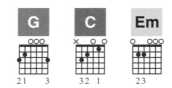

Verse
Moderately fast

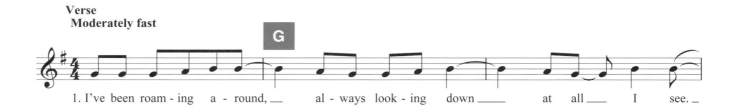

1. I've been roam-ing a - round, __ al - ways look-ing down __ at all __ I see. __

Paint - ed fac - es fill the plac - es I __ can't reach. __

You know __ that I could use some - bod - y. _____

You know __ that I could use some - bod - y, _____

some - one __ like you. __ 2. And all __ you know __ and how __ you speak. __
(3.) __ while you live it up, _____ I'm off __ to sleep, __

There's Nothing Holdin' Me Back

Words and Music by Shawn Mendes, Geoffrey Warburton, Teddy Geiger and Scott Harris

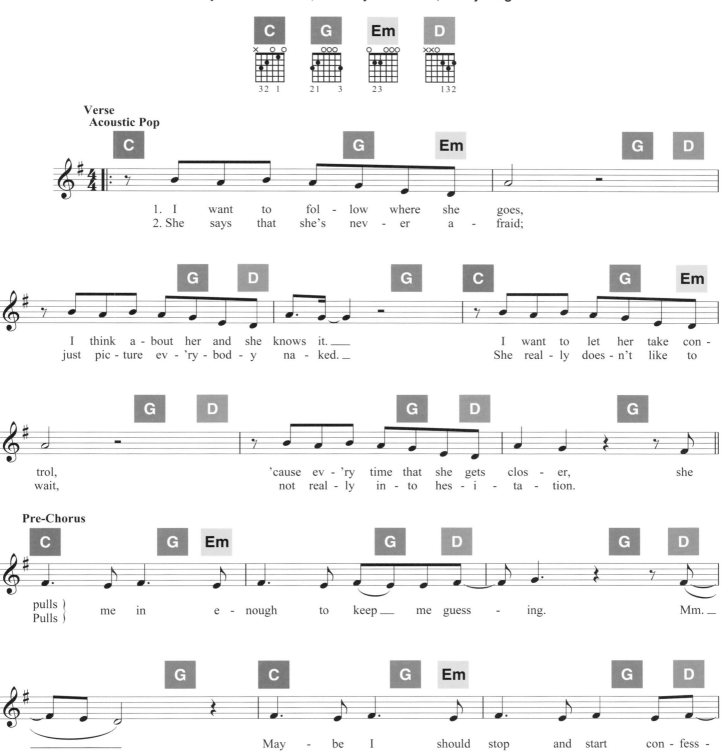

What About Us

Words and Music by Alecia Moore, Steve Mac and Johnny McDaid

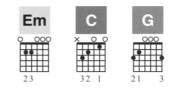

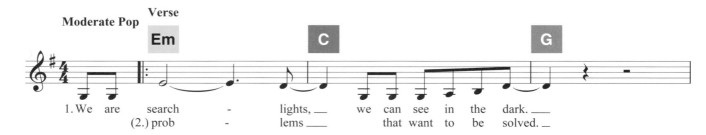

Moderate Pop — Verse

1. We are search - lights, __ we can see in the dark. __
(2.) prob - lems __ that want to be solved. __

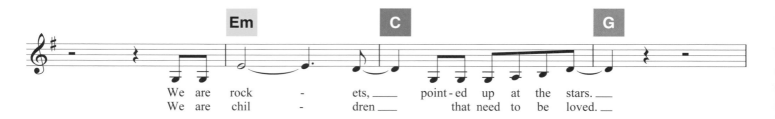

We are rock - ets, __ point - ed up at the stars. __
We are chil - dren __ that need to be loved. __

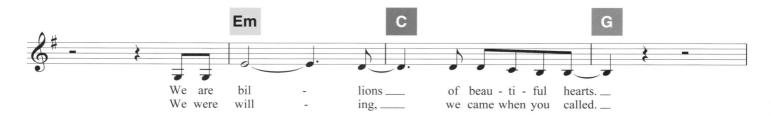

We are bil - lions __ of beau - ti - ful hearts. __
We were will - ing, __ we came when you called. __

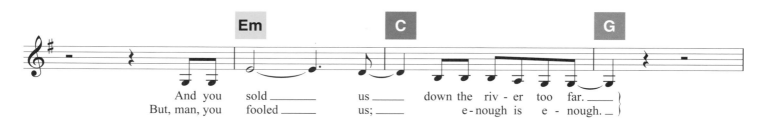

And you sold __ us __ down the riv - er too far. __)
But, man, you fooled __ us; __ e - nough is e - nough. __)

% Chorus

What a - bout us? What a - bout all the times you said you had the

an - swers?　　　　　　　What a - bout　us?　　　　　What a - bout

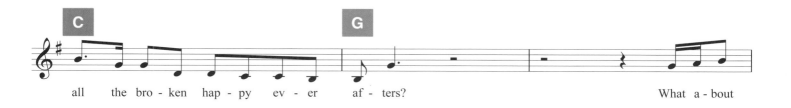

all　the bro - ken　hap - py　ev - er　af - ters?　　　　　　What a - bout

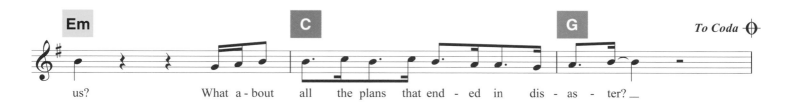

us?　　What a - bout　all　the plans that end - ed　in　dis - as - ter? __

What a - bout　love?　　　What a - bout ___ trust?　What a - bout ___

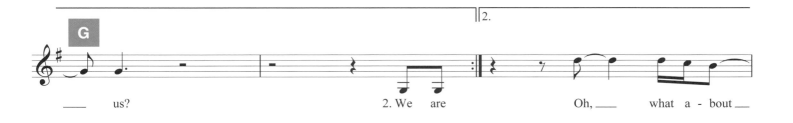

___ us?　　　　　　2. We are　　　Oh, ___ what a - bout ___

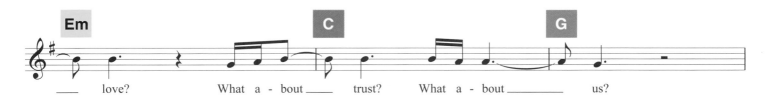

___ love?　　What a - bout ___ trust?　What a - bout ___ us?

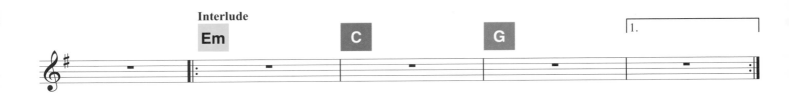

Interlude

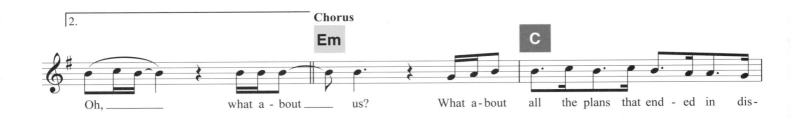

Chorus

Oh, _____ what a - bout _____ us? What a - bout all the plans that end - ed in dis-

as - ter? What a - bout love? What a - bout _

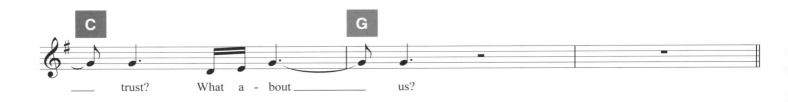

_____ trust? What a - bout _____ us?

Bridge

Sticks and_ stones,_ they may break these_ bones,_ but then I'll be read - y.
It's the _ start _ of us wak - ing __ up, _ come on. Are you read - y?

Are you read - y?
I'll be read - y. I don't want_ con - trol,_ I want_ to _ let go. _

Are you read - y? I'll be read - y. 'Cause now it's__ time__ to

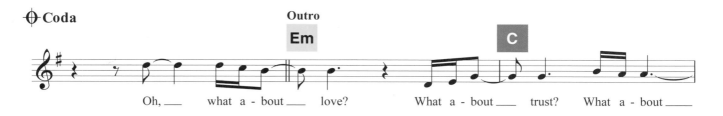

let them__ know._____ We are read - y.

What___ a - bout_____ us?

What a - bout_____

Oh,___ what a - bout___ love? What a - bout___ trust? What a - bout_____

___ us? What a - bout us?_____ What a - bout us?__

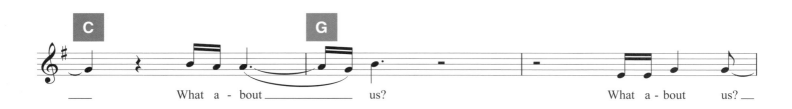

___ What a - bout_____ us? What a - bout us?__

___ What a - bout us?_____ What a - bout_____ us?

What Makes You Beautiful

Words and Music by Savan Kotecha, Rami Yacoub and Carl Falk

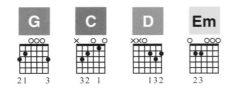

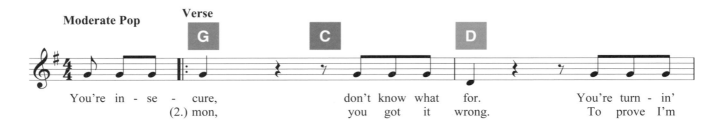

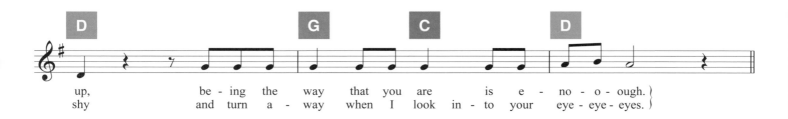

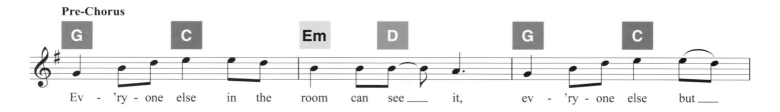

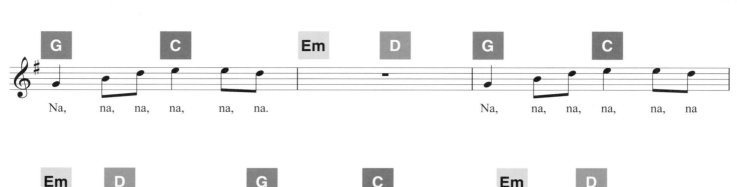

Na, na, na, na, na, na. Na, na, na, na, na, na

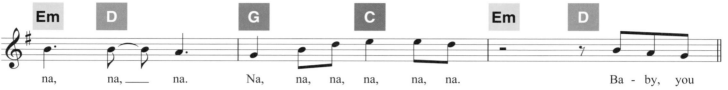

na, na, _____ na. Na, na, na, na, na, na. Ba - by, you

Chorus

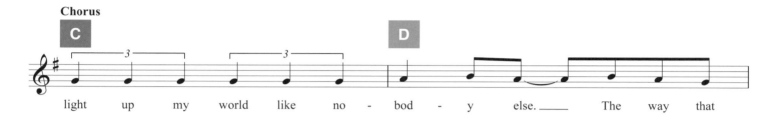

light up my world like no - bod - y else. _____ The way that

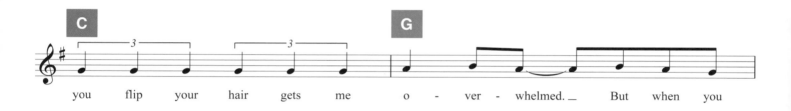

you flip your hair gets me o - ver - whelmed. _ But when you

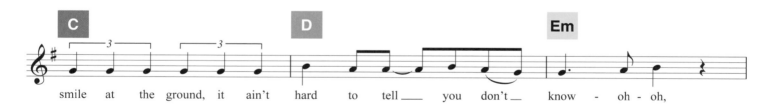

smile at the ground, it ain't hard to tell _ you don't _ know - oh - oh,

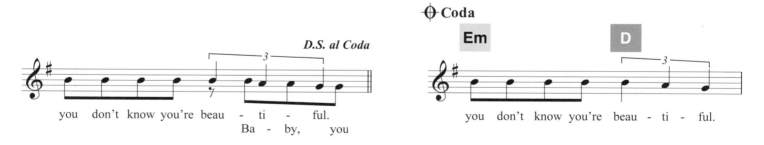

D.S. al Coda

you don't know you're beau - ti - ful.
Ba - by, you

Coda

you don't know you're beau - ti - ful.

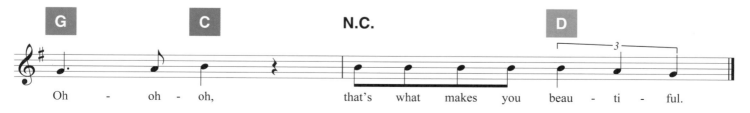

Oh - oh - oh, that's what makes you beau - ti - ful.

98

Thunder

Words and Music by Dan Reynolds, Wayne Sermon, Ben McKee,
Daniel Platzman, Alexander Grant and Jayson DeZuzio

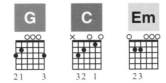

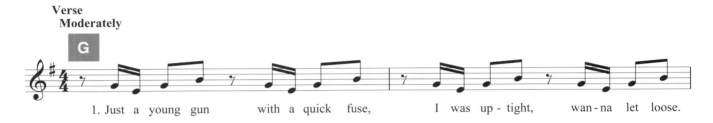

Thun - der,   thun - der, thun,   thun - der,   thu - thu - thun - der, thun - der.

Thun - der,   thun - der, thun,   thun - der,   thu - thu - thun - der, thun - der.

Chorus

Thun - der, ___   feel the thun - der, ___   light - ning and the thun - der. ___

To Coda ⊕

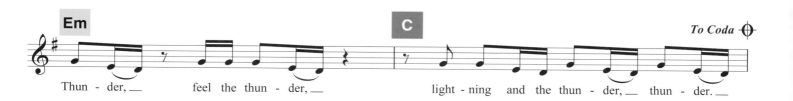

Thun - der, ___   feel the thun - der, ___   light - ning and the thun - der, ___ thun - der. ___

Thun - der. ___   Thun - der. ___

Verse

2. Kids were laugh - ing in my class - es while I was schem - ing for the mass - es.

"Who do you think you are dream-ing 'bout be-ing a big star?"

You say you're bas - ic, you say you're eas - y, you're al - ways rid - ing in the back seat.

D.S. al Coda

Now I'm smil - ing from the stage while you were clap - ping in the nose - bleeds.

Coda
Chorus

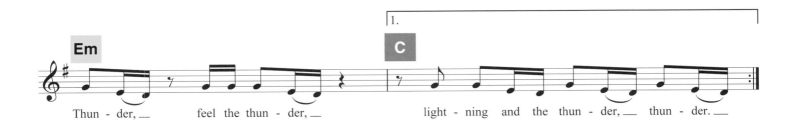

Thun - der, feel the thun - der, light - ning and the thun - der, thun - der.

1.

Thun - der, feel the thun - der, light - ning and the thun - der, thun - der.

2.

light - ning and the thun - der, thun - der.

STRUM AND PICK PATTERNS

This chart contains various patterns that can be used with songs in this book. The symbols ⊓ and ⌄ in the strum patterns refer to down and up strokes, respectively. The letters in the pick patterns indicate which right-hand fingers play which strings.

p = **thumb**
i = **index finger**
m = **middle finger**
a = **ring finger**

For example: Pick Pattern 2 is played: thumb - index - middle - ring.

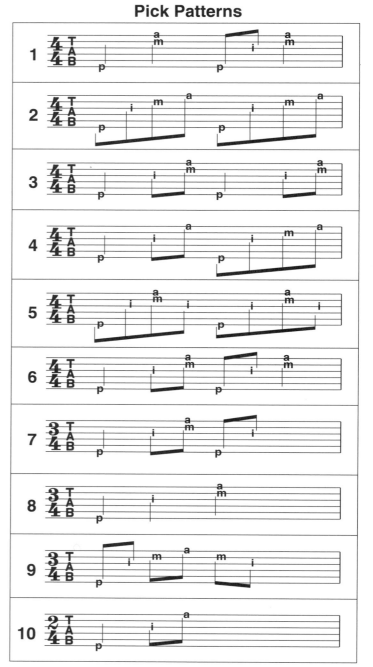

You can use the 3/4 Strum and Pick Patterns in songs written in compound meter (6/8, 9/8, 12/8, etc.). For example, you can accompany a song in 6/8 by playing the 3/4 pattern twice in each measure. The 4/4 Strum and Pick Patterns can be used for songs written in cut time (¢) by doubling the note time values in the patterns. Each pattern would therefore last two measures in cut time.